Are You an INSECT?

by **THOMAS KINGSLEY TROUPE**

amicus LEARNING

illustrated by **MARTINA ROTONDO**

Betty was a bumblebee. Two days ago at the zoo, someone said an odd word.

"I can't stand insects," Elijah the elephant said, swatting his tail.

"What's an insect?" Betty asked.

2

"Buzz off!" Elijah roared. "Bees are the worst!" He stomped away.

Betty couldn't just buzz off. She wanted to know.

Betty flew off to find insects. She asked Zoe the zebra.

ARE YOU AN INSECT?

"An insect?" Zoe laughed.

"Don't insult me. Most insects come from eggs. I was born alive!"

"So all insects lay eggs?"
Betty asked.

"Well, not all," Zoe said.
"Some beetles and aphids
and tsetse flies don't."

Betty made some notes.

At the underwater exhibit, she found Johnny the jellyfish.

"So, insects have more than one main body section?" Betty asked.

"They sure do," Johnny said. "They have three. A head, a thorax, and an abdomen."

Betty wrote that down.

Betty saw Randy the rat eating.

"Are you an insect?" she asked.
"Are you serious?" Randy asked. "I'm no insect, kid. I don't have compound eyes like most insects do."
"What are compound eyes?" Betty asked.
"They're eyes with lots of lenses that work together," Randy said. "They let insects see a wide view."

Betty added compound eyes to her notebook.

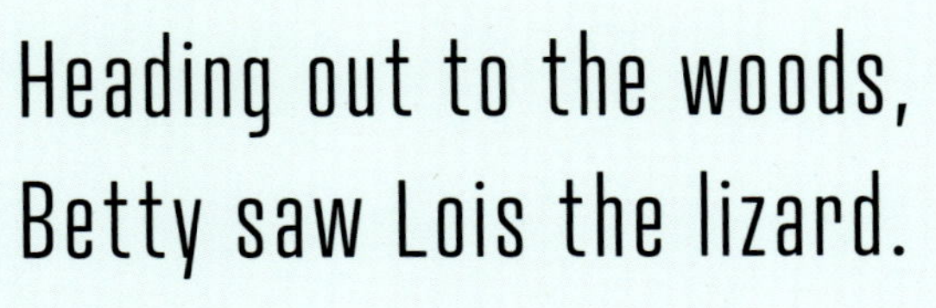

Heading out to the woods,
Betty saw Lois the lizard.

"An insect?"
Lois replied.

"Heavens no. Insects don't have
lungs. I need my lungs to breathe!"

"How do insects breathe?" Betty asked.

"Through openings called spiracles
in their abdomen and thorax!"

Betty added notes about spiracles.

11

Betty almost flew into Spike the
spider's web.

"Are you an insect?" Betty asked.
"No," Spike said. "I'm often called a bug
like insects, but I have eight legs."
"Insects don't have eight legs?"
Betty asked.
"Uh, no," Spike said. "All insects
have six legs."

Betty added six legs to her notes.

She spotted Hannah the hummingbird.

"An insect?" Hannah replied. "No, silly. Most flying insects have four wings."

"But you have wings," Betty said.

"Yes," Hannah said. "But birds only have two wings. A few insects, like flies and gnats, only have two wings, too."
Betty jotted down more notes.

Betty found Forrest the frog.

"Are you an insect?" Betty asked.
"Oh boy," Forrest said. "You're something else. No, I am not an insect! Do you see any antennae on my head?"
Betty looked. "No," she replied.
"That's because I don't have any," Forrest said. "All insects have two antennae for smelling and tasting."

Betty made notes about antennae.

Betty was getting tired. She saw Dexter the dragonfly.
"Hello?" Betty buzzed.

"You bet I am!" Dexter buzzed back. "I've got an exoskeleton like all adult insects."

"Finally!" Betty replied. "I found an insect! What's an exoskeleton?"

"It's a hard outer covering that protects insects' bodies," Dexter said. "Follow me!"

Betty followed Dexter. In the woods, she saw other insects with six legs. They each had a head, thorax, and abdomen. They had exoskeletons.

"Are you all insects?"
Betty asked.

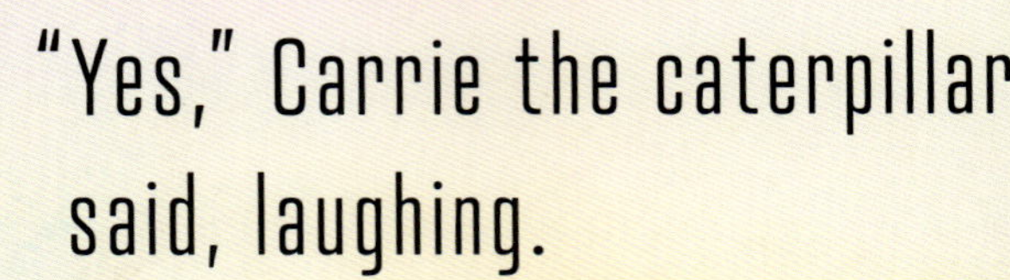

"Yes," Carrie the caterpillar said, laughing.
"And you are too!"

Betty looked at her reflection. She had two antennae!
She had six legs. She was an insect, too!

"I sure am," Betty said with a smile.

Betty's Notebook

INSECTS . . .

- Are usually hatched from eggs, except for some beetles and aphids and tsetse flies.

- Have three main body sections: a head, thorax, and abdomen.

- Do not have lungs. They breathe through holes in their bodies called spiracles.

- Have six legs. No more, no less.

- Usually have four wings, if they fly. A few, like flies and gnats, have only two wings.

- Have two antennae that act as sensory organs.

- Have an exoskeleton as adults.

GLOSSARY

abdomen The part of the body containing the digestive organs.

antennae Sensory organs located on the head of insects, used for touch and smell.

compound eyes Eyes made up of many lenses.

exoskeleton A hard covering that supports and protects the body.

head The part of an animal's body that contains the brain, most sensory organs, and the mouth.

spiracles Small holes for breathing in the side of an insect's body.

thorax The middle section of an insect's body where its wings and legs are attached.

WEBSITES

Arthropods | San Diego Zoo Animals and Plants

https://animals.sandiegozoo.org/animals/arthropods

BioKids — Kids' Inquiry of Diverse Species — Insects

http://www.biokids.umich.edu/critters/Insecta/

Invertebrates: National Geographic Kids

https://kids.nationalgeographic.com/animals/invertebrates

Every effort has been made to ensure that these websites are appropriate for children. However, because of the nature of the Internet, it is impossible to guarantee that these sites will remain active indefinitely or that their contents will not be altered.

READ MORE

Loy, Harriet. *Incredible Insects.* Bellwether Media: Minneapolis, 2023.

Peterson, Megan Cooley. *Tsetse Flies.* Black Rabbit Books: Mankato, Minn., 2023.

Vonder Brink, Tracy. *Insects.* Crabtree Publishing: New York, 2023.

AMICUS ILLUSTRATED is published by
Amicus Learning, an imprint of Amicus
P.O. Box 227, Mankato, MN 56002
www.amicuspublishing.us

Library of Congress Cataloging-in-Publication Data
Names: Troupe, Thomas Kingsley, author. | Rotondo, Martina, illustrator.
Title: Are you an insect? / Thomas Kingsley Troupe ; illustrated by Martina Rotondo.
Description: Mankato, MN : Amicus Illustrated, [2025] | Series: Animal classification | Includes bibliographical references. | Audience: Ages 6–9 | Audience: Grades 2–3 | Summary: "When young Betty the bumblebee hears Elijah the elephant complaining about insects, Betty sets out on a mission to find out what exactly an insect is. After interviewing other animals and learning about the characteristics of insects, Betty realizes that she too is an insect! Includes fact page, glossary, and resources for further research"— Provided by publisher.
Identifiers: LCCN 2024010606 (print) | LCCN 2024010607 (ebook) | ISBN 9798892001168 (library binding) | ISBN 9798892001748 (paperback) | ISBN 9798892002325 (ebook)
Subjects: LCSH: Insects—Juvenile literature. | Insects—Classification—Juvenile literature. | Animals—Classification—Juvenile literature.
Classification: LCC QL467.2 .T76 2025 (print) | LCC QL467.2 (ebook) | DDC 595.701/2—dc23/eng/20240404
LC record available at https://lccn.loc.gov/2024010606
LC ebook record available at https://lccn.loc.gov/2024010607

Printed in China

Editor: Rebecca Glaser
Designer: Kim Pfeffer

ABOUT THE AUTHOR

Thomas Kingsley Troupe is the author of more than 200 books for young readers. When he's not writing, he enjoys reading, playing video games, and investigating haunted places with the Twin Cities Paranormal Society. Otherwise, he's probably taking a nap or something. Thomas lives in Woodbury, Minnesota, with his two sons.

ABOUT THE ILLUSTRATOR

Artist since always, Martina Rotondo attended the Master of Illustration and Concept Art at The Sign Academy in Florence, Italy. She currently works as an illustrator for both Italian and foreign publishing houses. Lover of traditional drawing, she is also constantly researching and experimenting with new techniques to create her surreal and engaging characters and backgrounds.

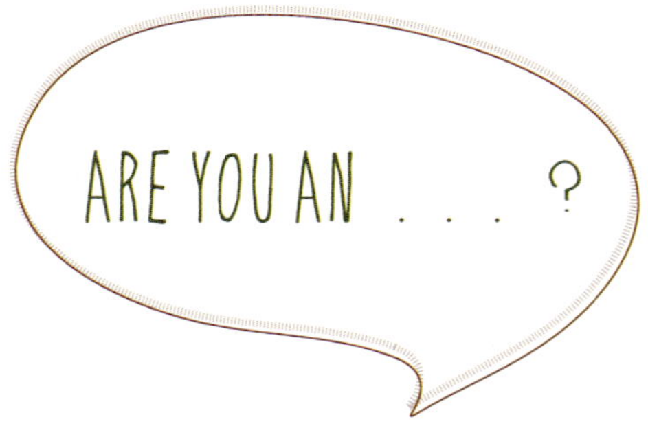